Lobstering

by Deborah Eaton

•

illustrated by
Rosanne Kaloustian

Scott Foresman

Editorial Offices: Glenview, Illinois • New York, New York
Sales Offices: Reading, Massachusetts • Duluth, Georgia
Glenview, Illinois • Carrollton, Texas • Menlo Park, California

I'm going to work with my father today.

I pull on an extra sweatshirt and my oldest, scruffiest shoes.

Other dads work in offices and stores. Mine works on a boat. He's a lobster fisherman.

"I'm ready," I whisper because my sisters are asleep.

Ma hands me a big lunch bag. Then she yawns. She's still in her bathrobe. That's because it's 4 A.M.

It's dark and quiet at the beach. It smells like seaweed and salt.

My father stops to talk to the other fishermen. He calls it "shootin' the breeze."

I try to carry the bait down to the water. It's salted redfish, packed in baskets. But my nine-year-old muscles just aren't strong enough. I drag the baskets. They make ridges in the wet sand.

My dad works hard. He even built our boat himself.

The BOB 'N' DEB.

She's named after me and my sisters. BOB is for my sister Bobbi. The N in the middle is Nancy. And I'm Deborah.

We call it "Bobbin' Deb."

The boat's not bobbing this morning. The water is still.

"Like glass," my father says. He lifts the bait baskets up into the boat. Then he starts the engine and pulls up the anchor.

I watch while the whole river turns silvery pink and orange. The sun is coming up.

Then the deck tilts under my feet.

This river is shallow. My dad has to navigate carefully here. The engine chug-chugs us out to the rollers at the river's mouth.

My dad revs the engine a little. Then we speed up. The big waves slap at the boat. Salt water sprays up in my face. It's cold. But it feels good. My dad grins. He likes it too. I can tell.

Once we're "outside"—out on the ocean—we head along the shore. That's where the lobsters are, among the rocks on the bottom.

I see one of my dad's buoys up ahead. I know it's his because it is white with an orange stripe. Lots of buoys float on the water here. Each one is attached by a rope to a lobster trap.

"Can I gaff the first one?" I ask. He hands me the gaff—a wooden pole with a hook on the end.

The boat slows.

There it is! I lean over the side and swing the gaff at the buoy rope. Got it on the first try!

"Pretty good, huh?" I say. But my dad is busy pulling on the rope. All his muscles strain to lift the heavy trap up out of the water.

The trap has two crabs, a starfish, and big bunches of seaweed in it. But there are no lobsters.

My dad puts more bait onto the hook. Then he fixes a bent wire on the underside.

He makes all his own traps in our basement. The hammer is always pounding down there.

My dad tips the trap back over the side of the boat. It pulls the heavy rope overboard super-fast—*zttt, zttt*. Drops of water spray from the rope where it rubs against the boat's side. They make a little rainbow. I lean over to watch.

A hand yanks my sweatshirt hard. I stagger back. My dad doesn't say anything. He just nods at the coil of rope near my feet.

Fishermen drown every year because they get a foot caught in a rope coil. They get yanked over the side.

My breath catches in my throat. I mutter, "Sorry." But my dad is already tossing the buoy overboard. And he's heading the boat to the next trap.

The next trap has one lobster inside.

Our first two dollars.

My dad checks to be sure the lobster is big
enough to keep. You have to measure. Then you
must throw the little ones back. That's for the
protection of all the lobsters, so there will always
be some left.

This one is a keeper.

I say, "Putting the bands on is my job, okay?"
I really want to help. My dad nods.

Rubber bands go around the claws to hold
them shut. Otherwise, the lobsters fight with
each other. They pull each other's claws right off.
That's no big deal to a lobster, I guess. If a
lobster loses a claw, it just grows another one.
But fishermen get paid by the pound. They want
to sell whole lobsters.

I pick up the lobster carefully, by its back. It
waves its claws at me.

The big claw has fat white teeth for crushing.
The smaller one has sharp little teeth for
tearing. I don't want either one getting near my
fingers, so I use a special tool to help put the
rubber bands on the lobster's claws.

You have to watch out for the tail too. The little flippers on the underside are sharp and the muscles are strong. Lobsters use that tail to swim. They open it, then flip it shut, fast. They scoot through the water—backward!

I slip rubber bands on both claws. I toss the lobster into a big barrel filled with salt water.

By now, we're already at the next trap.

After that, I can hardly keep up. We pull about ten more traps and get thirty lobsters, a few hermit crabs, and one dog shark. He's an ugly one. We'll use him for bait.

The next traps are in a "string"—four tied together on the same buoy. As the first one swings up out of the water, I can't believe it. There's a huge lobster in there. It's so big it has one claw stuck out the side!

"Hey! Look at that one!" I tell my dad. "You'll get so much money for him!"

But he shakes his head.

"I don't think so."

He turns the lobster over and shows me the underside. Little black beads coat all the ridges under the lobster's tail. It's a female with eggs. There are thousands of them.

My dad drops her back into the water. I watch as she sinks to the bottom. While she has eggs, we can't take her. It's another protection for the lobsters. So she gets away this time.

We pull about fifty traps. Then it's time to head home. Seagulls follow us, hoping for some left-over bait.

I start to clean down the boat with buckets of water and a big broom. But my dad can do it much faster. He takes over, while I hold the steering wheel steady. I stand on a box so I can see out the window.

We're home in time for a late lunch. I can hardly believe it. It feels as if we've been gone for a week. My arm muscles ache. The skin across my cheeks is tight and hot from windburn.

We all sit down at the kitchen table. Next thing I know, I'm jerking awake.

"Look!" says my sister Bobbi.

"She fell asleep in her spaghetti!" Nancy squeals, laughing.

"Hey, leave her alone," my dad says. "She worked hard today. Didn't you, Sis?" He winks at me and I feel my face flushing with pride.

My father is already finished eating. He heads out the door. I know where he's going. Pretty soon, we hear a hammer pounding in the cellar.